Left to right: David Bamford, Mason Goddard, David Simmons
Jean Taylor, Stephen Palmer, Phil Hewitson,
John S. Langley, Sherry Reidford.

Brampton Poets meet in Brampton Community Centre

CONTENTS

No Borders

John S. Langley

Nothing Stays the Same	3
Yellow	4
A Moment	6
Bystanders	7
Same Place, Different Time	9

Ena R. E. Hutchinson

Inspiration from "The Blue Box"	12
Listen	15

Jean Lawrie

False Impressions	18
See me? - or an Ode to Fashion	19
My Box	20

Matthew Taylor

For my son (on his sixth birthday)	22
Coming of Winter	25
Lost in The Amazon!	26
Morning Song	28

Ruth Kershaw

Whispering	32
Whispers	32
Balm	33

David Bamford

Seamus Heaney's Conway Stewart   36
Funeral   38
St Valentine's Day 2024   39
Being 80   40
Tranquillity   42

Ally Schofield

Don't look at us like cake   46
Look through our eyes   48
Hearing or not   50
The Ballad of an Out-of-reach Life   52
Lest we forget   55

Geoff Smith

Cumbrian Haiku   58 - 61

Kat van Hookens

Mums Only!   64
The Repugnant Potion   66
Who'll weep for the trees?   67
You gotta love a lolly   68
Mud's Thicker than Blood   71

Stuart Turner

Urban Observations, June 2024   74
To The Hills   77
Suli's Dream   78
Talkin', Walkin'   80
Money saving   81

Katie Evans

County man   84
Altiplà, San Elordi   85
Word Witch   86
Chronology of Rona   88

Stephen Palmer

Haiku Calendar   90
Carol   92
Dementia   94
Our window cleaner   96
Grassland   98

Jean Taylor

Ken 99 Ice Cream Party   102
WRNS   104
Blue   106
Roots   108

Philip Brown

In Vain I Search Your Face   110
Here, Just Here   111
The Longer Way   112
Andromeda   113
Winter's Wood   116

Mary Thornton

Alphabet for geriatrics   120
Folding you in my heart   121
A New Meaning for Provocative!!   122
Thoughts on Death   124
The Standing Stone   125

David Simmons

Wiser than boundaries (after Tony Hendry)   128
Shoulders broader than borders   130
Three Haiku   131

Mason Goddard

What a world   134
Love me like a swan   135
Ultraviolet   136
Andromeda   137

Jane Moss-Luffrum

Theft   140
Achieving symmetry   143
We moved her in   144
Somos Luz   145
The dog walk   146

Phil Hewitson

Papillon   150
Ever Present Presence   151
Aurora Night   152
My Beautiful Shadow   154
Parting Words   155

Dear Reader   157

No Borders

For Brampton Poets 2024 began soon after the book launch of our fifth anthology *Beyond Borders*, with Katie Evans the first poet featured in the new 'monthly poem' display in the reception of Brampton Community Centre. Members of the group have taken part in various local events across the year including; a very busy Spark educational day at Shankhill CofE Primary School, joining Phil Furneaux to plant several trees with Brampton 2 Zero (thanks to David Simmons' suggestion to sponsor trees), and the successful 'popup' bookshop (both at Talkin Tarn) instigated by Geoff Smith.

During this time conflicts sadly continue around the world, elections produced unusual results with populist candidates swept to power, high profile figures (including members of the royal family) revealed they were receiving treatment for various illness, commemorations marked the 80th D-Day anniversary, a global software update knocked computers offline, Paris held triumphant Olympic and Paralympic Games, the England men's football team got to the final of the Euros to face favourites Spain, we saw civil unrest and riots brought under control, and the magical spectacle of the Northern Lights appeared across the UK, and many parts of the world which rarely see the aurora.

We do live in interesting times and many pieces inspired by these events feature in this new collection *No Borders*.

David Bamford also stepped back from his various chair roles with Brampton Poets, we thank him for all he's done. The group continues, now meeting in the craft room at the community centre, to share the magic of poetry. Our first collection was made possible by a charitable donation and we continue with our not-for-profit remit to donate to local charities with a portion of our profits. We hope our readers enjoy these latest works.

Phil Hewitson, on behalf of Brampton Poets.

John S. Langley, poet, author and enthusiastic reader

John S. Langley

John Langley was born and raised in the North East of England and has two brothers, three sons but only one wife. After qualifying as a Chemical Engineer he was lucky enough to work around the world on various projects before moving into Consultancy and finally becoming his own company.

Latterly he has managed to achieve a BA and an MA in Creative Writing from the Open University and is author or contributor to more than 15 books ranging from Crime novels and Children's books to Poetry and is a member of several writing groups from which he continues to learn.

John acted as compiler, editor (with help from several others) and publisher of the first four Brampton Poets Anthologies and is thankful to have now been able to hand over the reins.

John, Kat and Stephen see the funny side

Nothing Stays the Same

The place I was conceived in has been knocked down
The pub I was born in has changed its name
My first secondary school is no more
I'm beginning to get a complex

Houses I called home are now occupied by strangers
Family and friends are scattered in the winds
'You can't go back, so much is true
Even though it's part of you.'

Each cell in my body has been systematically replaced
Every seven years or so, a remarkable process
I'm not the same person I used to be
Maybe that's a good thing…

Yellow

*This poem may only be for people of a certain age when
Iodine solution was supplied in small bottles with droppers
for use as an antiseptic. Drops were either put direct onto
the wound or put onto a piece of cloth or cotton wool and
then dabbed on – each method was equally painful!*

When I was young
at least one of my knees
was always yellow

Wearing shorts was the thing
saving the wear and tear on clothing
by exposing the knees

It seemed that everything
worth doing involved
falling and scraping

You got used to the sight
of your own red blood
and the repair process

the wound drying, scabbing, itching
scratching, then repeating the errors
new scabs for old

The new skin was diaphanous pink
baby smooth and wrinkle-free
needing light and air

But the thing I remember most
was the sting of the Iodine
the yellowing of the skin

Yeow! It was worse than the wound
A caring mother's method
of combating infection

I came to believe that bright yellow
was the natural colour of
a young boy's knees

Because, when I was young
at least one of my knees
was always yellow

A Moment

of contentment
takes me
by surprise

The quiet, the tang
of salt
upon my tongue

The waves rolling
in breaking lines
of white

The sea, silver
in reflected
light

The sky, blue
air still
and fresh

A feeling
of calm sweeps
over me

A fleeting moment
of welcome
respite

As I turn away
I promise myself
I'll remember
moments like this.

Bystanders

We are observers
Of other people's trials
From a distance

Intellectually dissecting
Other people's distress
Looking on

It only really matters
When it is our trauma
Our pain

When that world is
All of a sudden, ours
With no escape

Then we don't understand
Why everyone else doesn't
Feel our pain as we do

Why there is no outpouring
Of sensible, practical action
To stop each other hurting

But that is not the way.

We look on
From a distance
Expert bystanders…

A moment in the 'Debateable Lands' between Hadrian's Wall and the current Scottish Border.

Same Place, Different Time

Here, before mankind
Green tropical forests flourished
Amidst a rich hum of insect wings

Here, heavy footprints were left
Hard skinned beasts in charge
Masters for millennia

Here, ice lay, many meters thick
Cleansing all that had gone before
Erasing the writing on an old page

Here, forests rose again, rivers ran
And the hand of man first lay
Upon the rough bark

Here, fires raged, tools were made
Crops were sown, children grew
And passed on their knowledge

Here, in this now quiet spot I stand
A passing shadow in dappled sunlight
Caught within a breeze

Ena R. E. Hutchinson, poet

Ena R. E. Hutchinson

Ena was born in Harrogate Golf Club in 1936 where her parents were living as Steward and Stewardess. During World War II Ena, a younger brother and two young cousins were all brought up together as one family, with grandparents and an aunt, while the fathers were serving abroad.

On leaving secondary school, Ena attended Harrogate Technical College for Catering. Leaving there at 16, she undertook a two-year managerial course in London with J Lyons & Co. before returning to Yorkshire to be with her grandmother after her grandfather's death. Ena married her first husband in 1958 and had two sons and, later, six grandchildren and a great-granddaughter.

With a career as a self-employed caterer, Ena moved north to Preston in 1964 and then to the Borders. In the early 1980s, Ena ran the Cathedral Buttery – as it was in those days.

Ena met Gilbert in 1985. They were married in 1986 and moved to Brampton in 2002. They shared a love of walking, nature, books and music, and Ena came to appreciate poetry. Following trips to The Theatre By The Lake in early 2016, the idea of a Brampton Poets group formed and, following encouragement, was launched.

Inspiration from "The Blue Box"

*Century Theatre was founded just after World War Two and
toured the country in a pop-up space pulled by trucks. It
eventually broke down in a Derwentwater Lakeside car
park where it remained for many years and became affec-
tionately known as 'The Blue Box'. It directly led on to the
campaign for the creation of the 'Theatre by the Lake' and a
permanent home for theatre in Keswick.*

The Blue Box is a treasure beyond compare,
Such a joy to have found over 40 years ago.
It holds the most amazing gifts and a store
of untold exciting times.

So many times shared with family and friends.
Meetings arranged to share coffee, lunch or
afternoon teas. The music, the plays, the pantos
that came from the beloved Blue Box.

Such entertainment, such fun and laughter.
The strolls to the Lake, picnics, games on the grass
Or a sail down the Lake to alight at Barrow House
and walk back through the woods to Friars Crag
walking by the moored boats to the dear Blue Box.

You have served us well over the many years,
but as we sat amid buckets, to capture the water
when it rained, we feared that the end was nigh!
Your body old and beyond repair, but your soul

is alive and will live on - The Blue Box is no more

but the legacy you left is the 'Theatre by the Lake'
giving us all the gifts as before. It's now watertight
and offers everyone so much more.

What a privilege to be invited to a whole weekend,
looking around the theatre before opening new doors
once more. Stage, dressing rooms, down in the pit,
up overhead and views from the flies. All a special thrill.

Sitting in a box before opening day, an experience
to treasure. Inspiration later when Brampton Poets
was born – all from the 'Blue Box', now 'Theatre by
the Lake' and their introduction of 'Words by the Water'.

that sowed the seeds and set minds ticking
Thank you my DEAR OLD BLUE BOX...

St Martin's Church

Listen

This poem I wrote recently. Our church bells ceased to chime during lockdown. They have just begun to ring again and on hearing them these words came to me…

Listen   I hear the peel of the bells as they call out
               saying all is well, have no fear.
      I hear the voice of the Saviour saying
      "I am holding you in the palm of my hand
      All I ask is your love and to love your neighbour,
        Come put your hand into mine"
         Ding Dong,
              Ding Dong,
                     Ding

      Can you hear them singing?
      "Come I am waiting"… listen… to the strike
      of each melodious sound
         Let it echo in your heart

Jean Lawrie, poet

Jean Lawrie

Born in Edinburgh in 1933, Jean had three older brothers. At six years old she was evacuated to a farm in Inverness-shire during the Second World War. Back home, she attended the local primary school, then Portobello High School. Jean left school knowing what she wanted to do and what she didn't want to do. No chance of drama school! Her father suggested radiography, so as something different Jean went along with that. Four years after qualifying she married, became pregnant immediately and had to give up work. Within five years she was a mother of four children. Her husband worked in his father's business until he bought a shop of his own. When he sold that they moved into a bed and breakfast. Ten years later they retired and spent two years touring America in a motorhome. Back home they had to take on her mother-in-law and moved to Livingstone. Her husband Jim died in 2004 and she lived alone with visits from family until she came to Brampton Court where she imagines she'll live happily ever after.

False Impressions

Here's a good one of you Mum
Said my son
Handing me a photograph
of a fat old woman.

'Me? Thats never me!
I'm not that fat
I'm not that old'

Yet she's wearing my clothes
She's sitting in my chair
I've been told the camera never lies
(though it certainly exaggerates)
so I suppose she must be me.

Oh dear, when did my perception of myself
stray so far from the reality?
Still as I always say
It's how you feel that counts.

See me? - or an Ode to Fashion

Ma hair is as red as the settin sun
Ma lips as black as the night.
Ah've rings oan ma fingers an' rings on ma toes.
Cos see me? Ahm a punk rocker.

Silver balls run round the curves o my ears
A dozen oan each side
Take them aw oot ma da allege
an you'll be left wi serrated edges
See him? He kens ah'm a punk rocker.

Ah've a stud juttin oot frae unner ma lip
Ma tongue cradles aven another.
But if ah lose this one like the one before
Ah'll no bother wi ony more,
Even though ah'm a punk rocker.

A butterfly flies across ma back
Wings spread frae shoulder to shoulder.
Ah've lots of tattoos dotted here and there
But then, see me? Ah'm a punk rocker.

Now, achieving this look is no sae easy
It costsa lot of money ye ken.
An' folks who say "Pride feeleth no pain"
Dinna ken what they are sayin
Cos see me? Ah'm worth it.

My Box

My box is a beautiful blue
Enamelled with Winnie the Pooh
Ballooning high into the sky
Far from the earth below.

This box is a box of dreams gone by
Of a life that was thrilling and free
Of a space in time that belonged to us
A time to simply be.

My box of blue is not alone
Others stand alongside on that shelf
Each one contains a memory
Each one a piece of myself.

Matthew Taylor

Not a native of Cumbria, Matthew has lived in or around Brampton for 15 years.

He says, 'I've enjoyed writing since a very early age. I like to write poems when the mood takes, but I've also written a few unpublished novels and stories. I often find the countryside around Brampton an inspiration for what I write, whilst the human condition is an inexhaustible source of material and I find poetry an outlet to probe and examine it.'

For my son (on his sixth birthday)

Carry on until the utmost of your hours
There's a resting place
Nested in pleasant flowers

But till that moment, for you the blasted wind
And the swirling sleet
Will be the whited foil
To stir you from your sleep

Go onwards, towards your gallant future toils
Where deeds, however small or meek
Shall at the turning of the day
Be rewarded by the gains of all you seek

Fear naught, for fear is a friend to your foes
And they would use your dread
To twist the twine of inaction
And bind your hands behind your head

You are the brilliance of stars
For you they were cast
In the elemental fire of their majesty
And from them is made
The atomic patten of your mind,
A mind so magnificent it can prick
The petty gods to envy

Perhaps one day you may swirl
The very essence of life
And make great scientific findings
Or weave a cloth of gold,
Who knows,
With a genius for paint or writings

You are still so small
Yet even now you push
An inquisitive mind
Into the darkened corners of this world
And by probing, I see,
The sticky thread of life
Is a silk of comprehension you've unfurled

But later when in adulthood,
Do not let others grub you
Into thinking your motives
Are ignoble
It is always right to ask them for their proof
And always worth the trouble

Yet worry not if you find truth
Is searing bright
For knowledge will sometimes
Scratch your vision
With its blinding light

Be good
Be gentle
Respect others
Even those whose aim
Is to make you a fool
For they will only be led to wisdom
If you use your confidence as a tool

Be magnanimous in triumph
Do not gloat on weaker men
Nor yet be humiliated in defeat
Have the courage to start again

You may win or lose
A game or two
But remember
Victory goes
To he who sees it through

Your existence is a river rushing on
To the ocean's salty halt
And on that journey
You will know the wide world
With all its goodness and its faults

There will be challenges
Throughout your lifetime's span
But remember it is the kindness
You show
My son
That will turn you into a man.

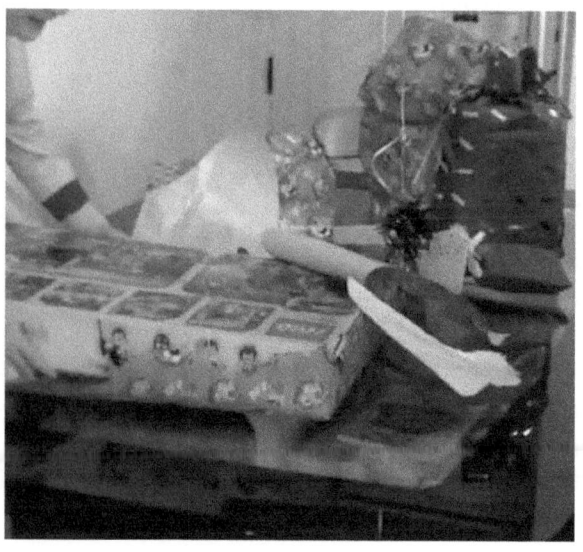

Coming of Winter

I suppose all seasons have their beauty
Even the most gloomy
Even the most irrepressibly dark
Even those with the coldest heart.

And so I look around, look up
And spy a song bird singing in the larch
But I think 'are you well wrapped up?'
And 'will I see you come next March?'

I ask her 'Do you fear the coming snow
Do you fear the biting hail
Or are you ignorant of your fate
And all it might entail?

Do you live but for the moment
For this very minute now?
And are all your hours mapped out
With what nature will allow?'

Oh I hope you do not know
I hope you can't foresee
How Winter may bring its breath of death
To the likes of you and me.

Lost in The Amazon!

I care not
I care not
For material things
The stuff that next day
Delivery brings
It's always plastic
Always trite
And often breaks
When dropped from height.

There is a case for making do
And mending things that
Aren't quite new
Much better that than - to put it mild -
Work to death a third-world child.

Oh I know.
It's too easy isn't it.
To click on this and 'Alexa' that.
To greet with a crescendo of childish glee
The parcel that's addressed: to ME!
Like a birthday delivered to your home
A self-bought present in wrapping foam.
(My God, how they love that foam!)

But think! Dear God, Man. Think aloud
Let your thoughts connect
It doesn't tally that the more you have
The more you have self-respect
(Quite the opposite, in fact)

Put down the iPad, put down the phone
Cancel Click and Collect
Go out and breathe God's clean air
Before the planet's wrecked!

*In an effort to help do our bit to combat the
environmental crisis 'before the planet's wrecked'
David Bamford, David Simmons, Phil Hewitson, Ena Hutchinson,
on behalf of Brampton Poets, plant trees at Talkin Tarn in
spring 2024 - in collaboration with B2Z (Brampton 2 Zero)
and Phil Furneaux - as part of a tree planting
carbon neutral initiative.*

Morning song

Wake up! wake up!
The green goddess is here
With her auburn hair
And pastel lips
Spreading the sun
With her finger tips
Playing out
The first note
Of bird song
In her throat

Wake up! wake up!
Milking cows barrel
Out from the parlour;
Their baritone
Calls
Echo the past
As they chorus the wind
Across the grass

Wake up! wake up!
The crows
On their busy commute
Caw caw
As they swoop
And ignore
The prudish daylight
To breakfast
On those
Who did not make it
Through the night

Ruth Kershaw, poet

Ruth Kershaw

Ruth has lived in Brampton for 50 years. She was born in Rochdale, but, due to her father's promotions on the railway, found herself in Halifax by the time she was 10. Here she stayed until she had gained School Certificate. Now at the northern end of the chain, Ruth thinks of herself as a Pennine woman and revels in their wildness. She has walked the Pennine Way.

A long period of bedrest (age 6 rheumatic fever) gave time to indulge in Arthur Mee's encyclopaedia, the Poetry and Natural History sections laying foundation for lifelong interests.

She is indebted to her English teacher for encouraging her to write essays but did not venture into poetry until 2013 when she enjoyed a Poetry Course at Stones Barn, Roweltown, North Cumbria, led by Ian Duhig. Immediately "hooked" she has attended two more of the same.

A retired Methodist Minister, she finds poems easier than sermons.

Whispering

(the pleasure and the pain
- a quirky ballad?)

Darling
"I love you"
he whispered
in her ear.

She blushed.

Years later
she whispered
some idle news
to her friend.

Bringing pain

Whispers

eventually
i got the message
delayed by
Chinese whispers

Balm

Far from calm
in pain and alarm
he squirmed in pain
relief to gain

Then in came John
from ages gone
to cheer him on
to hope again

And do you know
you'd never guess
the balm of love
and happiness
did give him cause
to hope once more

David Bamford, poet

David Bamford

David Bamford considers himself an honorary Cumbrian, in that his wife was born in Penrith, his children were born in Kendal and he lives in Brampton. He has been a member of Brampton Poets since the group's inception, has participated in the delivery of workshops and in performances of his work.

David is also a self-published author of five books in his own right.

He is delighted to be involved in the creation of this sixth collection of Brampton Poets' work, which provides evidence that the Muse continues to burn (if that's what muses do).

Seamus Heaney's Conway Stewart

A few years ago, I visited the Seamus Heaney Home Place in Bellaghy, Northern Ireland. There, in a glass case in the atrium which formed the entry to a museum of the poet's life and work, was his fountain pen, a Conway Stewart, the Rolls Royce of writing implements. What a privilege to behold the tool that had crafted, immortalised so many gems of literature that had flowed from the brain and the hand of this 'extraordinary man in ordinary clothes'.

A fountain pen is just a pen,
a tool with which to write.
Mightier, maybe, than the sword.
That depends upon the hand
that holds it, wields it.
It may exalt, condemn, insult or praise,
immortalise.

A Conway Stewart is not just any fountain pen.
It is a pen of class,
and Seamus Heaney's Conway Stewart
is not just any Conway Stewart.
It's a pen that crafted words of genius.

I saw it once,
reclining in a case of glass
Home Place, Bellaghy,
That's where it was.
The shrine preserves the poet's memory, his words,
his Conway Stewart,
a Concorde among fountain pens,

lying quiet, not writing now,
but oh! what memories may it conjure?
What rivers flowed from that golden nib
to earn the poet recognition,
adulation,
immortality,
making extraordinary the ordinary,
the everyday,
the commonplace.

Seamus Heaney's Conway Stewart.
A pen among, yet far above,
so many others.

Funeral

*On 1st May, I took part in the funeral of someone for whom
I had developed a strong affection and respect. I had taken
Communion to her on a monthly basis during the last years
of her life until shortly before her death. I had visited her a
few times, watching her gradually slipping away. It was an
honour to be asked to read and give an address at the ser-
vice.*

Stones of muted tones
somewhere between
beige and brown.
A peppering of sunlight
filtered through stained glass,
splashing clothes and pews
with dabs of light.

Muffled voices punctuate the silence
as family, mourners, a congregation
who loved the one who is no longer here,
nor will be any more
exchange greetings, words of comfort.

The organ adds its tactful drone –
Pachelbel, if I'm not mistaken –
and men in black enter with the coffin,
place it on a frame.

Then those well-known words,
'I am the resurrection and the life...'

The service runs its course.
Then brilliant sunshine greets us
in the churchyard,
the fullness of spring at noon
for the committal.

Is this how life must end,
in a box in a hole
in the ground?
For mortal remains maybe,
But is there more beyond?
A higher glory that we will never know
while we remain
here on earth?

St Valentine's Day 2024

A thought for what is a special day in so many people's lives

Love speaks, but often not with words,
for words are often not enough.
A look,
just a glance,
a touch,
a feather's soft caress
may be all you need,
especially today.

Being 80

Roger Daltry is considerably better known than I will ever be. The one thing we have in common is that we were born in the same year, 1944. On turning 80, he wrote, 'what the f*** am I still doing here? I'm in the way. All us old farts. We really are just in the way of the young now, aren't we?' Also, 'who the f*** wants to be 80?' When I turned 60, I was pleased. I determined then to rejoice in every '0. I did so when I reached 70, now here's the next one. It may well be the last.

My father did not live till eighty.
He died not two weeks short
of seventy-five,
on my birthday,
one I won't forget.
I turned forty-five that day,
five years past the half-way point
between my birth and now.
The years I've lived since then have been a gift
to treasure,
cherish
and look after.

How?
Living modestly,
avoid excess.
Alcohol I do not touch
much
a glass of wine from time to time,
sometimes before I go to bed,

a snifter ... just to help me sleep
you understand
early to bed
to rise as well,
forty minutes on my static bike
before I face the day.

How much longer do I have?
I've no idea.
I hope I'll occupy the time
in such a way
that when that time is done
I'll be glad to think
that it's been worth it.

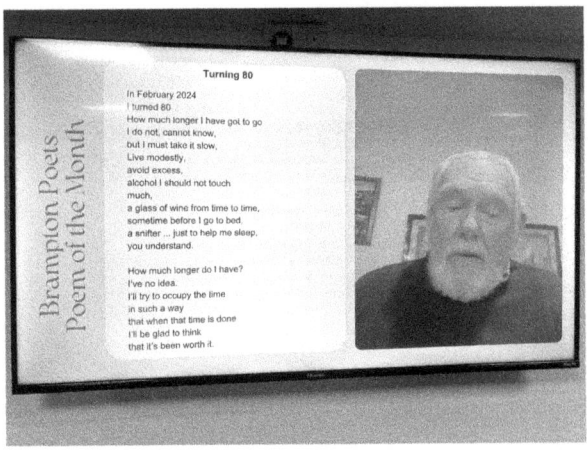

*In 2024 Brampton Poets began sharing monthly poems which
are displayed on screen and notice board in the
reception at Brampton Community Centre*

*Pictured is David Bamford reading 'Turning 80'
for February 2024*

Tranquillity

Walking one day in April along the Hadrian's Wall Path, I was stuck by the splendour and beauty of nature, the absolute stillness of the air. There was not the breath of a breeze, and, after the foulness of a bitter, over-long winter, Spring had entered its fullness.

Above, the sky,
blue,
dabbed with white
fleece-fluff clouds
in languid motion,
mirrored in miniature below
by lazing, grazing sheep,
guardians of their lambs
that frisk and stray
but never far
from maternal care,
concern
and tenderness.

A landscape
traversed by a wall
of massive masonry,
huge, implacable,
motionless,
eloquent in its impassivity.

Birds wheel above
No sound,
unless it be

the muffled hum,
the whine
of a distant passing car.

Tranquillity

Ally Schofield, poet, singer, artist

Ally Schofield

Having spent most of my 36 years in Gloucestershire, I moved to Carlisle 5 years ago. I was found to be deaf when I was six, with a progressive bi-lateral hearing loss, and over the years other health conditions have emerged. At the beginning of 2024 I was finally diagnosed with a very rare genetic condition called ACPHD (Ataxia Cerebellar and Peripheral, Hearing Loss and Diabetes). I also had a close encounter with critical illness nearly two years ago, which has given me a heightened appreciation for the things and people around me. I feel it is important to share with people my struggles and joys in life, to give them greater insight, and hopefully to help other people who might find themselves in similar situations. I also enjoy writing poetry about nature, and things close to my heart.

Don't look at us like cake

When they looked at me;
it wasn't me they saw.
They saw a cake half eaten;
but I am so much more.

When people hear 'disabilities';
no matter what they are;
some immediately assume;
'that person won't get far'

They decide they know
if we are capable or not.
But believe me;
- that is utter rot.

We are individuals;
With different strengths to yours.
And we are just as deserving
of newly-opened doors.

So to be a better person;
kind and not opaque;
Think twice before assuming,
and don't look at us like cake.

Our qualities shout out loudly;
And we see things another way;
Oh, we can really shine;
If you listen to what we say.

So instead of fearing disabilities;
Value the gifts we bring.
Celebrate our differences;
And give us a song to sing.

Look through our eyes

We see a different world –
Yours is straight – ours is curled
Among bungalows just one skyscraper
Or think of a lonely sheet of paper,
A blank page, white as snow.
Unknown land where new things grow

Your view of things to us is unclear
On the paper, only outlines appear
– they are thick like charcoal.
We quite easily fall down a hole
It gives us chaos, adding shade
And we're unnerved when clarity fades
Layers will give us more confusion
Which ends up with our exclusion

We are many – but all too often
Others treat us with worried caution
We get left in shadows on our own
to be different – is to be alone.

It does not make us any less
Our feelings we can still express
We find beauty that others don't –
And see the things that they won't
the hidden jewels reach our eyes,
It can be a blessing in disguise

But really we are the same as you;
we just have a different view.

Just as people have different opinions
And a person has their own dominion
So please don't run
And before you shun,

Before you make our beating hearts sink
Hold your horses – Stop and think.
Consider what it is you imply
And try to look through our eyes.

Hearing or not

I don't know who came to the door;
But I'd never seen them before.
I don't know if they had a double chin;
I certainly didn't invite them in.

They wore an invisibility cloak,
There weren't any puffs of smoke.
They waved an invisible magic wand,
To steal my hearing and abscond;
But those intentions were unclear
Until sound faded from each ear.

Stony silence was left behind;
Like a blockage in my mind.
The invisible stranger and my hearing;
Finished their act by disappearing.
Their very presence was lost in a crowd;
Their arrival was quiet; their leaving loud.

Not loud in the normal sense of the word;
Not a huge noise that can be heard.
I opened the door not knowing what I'd lose;
And there was no one there to let me choose.
There was no prior knowledge to act upon;
It was when they'd left, I knew they'd gone.

Things then became unspoken,
For my original ears were broken;
And there was nothing to help them mend;
So silence became my very good friend.

Grown ups are aware of potential thieves,
Now I have an eye on people's sleeves;
Just in case of hidden tricks,
But back then I was only six.

Now, I would not change what came before;
I don't let trials become a chore.
For I am me, Sir: Ma'am,
And I am proud of who I am.

To be clear: for my hearing I do not grieve,
But hearing aids they can deceive.
People say they comprehend,
That sounds together often blend.
What we hear can be confused,
And we feel quite bemused.
But do people really understand
Unless they've experienced it first-hand?

The Ballad of an Out-of-reach Life

I woke from a deep sleep,
Not knowing I was me.
It should have been a cheerful day.
But I was still at sea.

The bright lights attacked like punches
With the clarity of mud.
Before I know the guilt is there
It hits me with a thud.

I'd travelled through the dark,
On my journey home.
People were all around,
But I was still alone.

Though they took the tube,
The silence still was mine.
Everything seemed wrong,
I failed to reach the line.

For now stop the clocks,
They mean nothing; time or day.
The past would not have happened,
Had there been another way.

My mouth will not form words;
I have some questions you know.
The thoughts in my head are stuck,
They have nowhere else to go.

I look up at no sky,
I look around at sea.
Distant land, are you there?
But there is only me.

Each visiting time would come,
When my hands in theirs were clasped,
But my paws; they remained useless,
My mitts; they would not grasp.

The smiles I recognised,
Hour on hour as I lay.
What's the point in asking why?
And I can't anyway.

And what of outside?
I can't ask anyone you know.
Is there a patter of rain?
Or a light dusting of snow?

I know winter still dominates,
And the festivities already left.
I remained in their hurry,
And I feel a bit bereft.

So I imagine the sky,
The blue unclouded weather,
But the light is unnaturally bright,
Like candles burning together.

Now back inside my head,
Warm sun rays fall on me.

The salty refreshing spray,
Of the desolate forlorn sea.

I'm told I'm doing well
And hopefully winning my fight.
Then his words come out of the blue,
A sword in a cloud of light.

But now my hands; they work,
On the bad I must not dwell.
My mind grows ever more sharp
And now I can finger spell.

Push back I must, when I see
Shadows of the world appear.
The road home is faint,
But the riddle becomes more clear.

Rough terrain on a dark night,
Is the road I have not taken.
If you see this as the end,
Then you are much mistaken.

I will ride these waves of lifeless sea,
The laid out miles of strife.
I'll meet with land once more,
And bring this ocean to life.

I sail the sea for days in my head,
Wishing, hoping, and then;
Three cheers I say; land ahoy!
For my voice is back again.

Lest we forget

We give our thoughts
to those who were lost,
For never once
did they count the cost,
They fought with bravery
of the utmost,
And the courage they showed
at their post,
Is something none
will ever forget,
And we will always be,
in their debt,
We give them special silence
on the hour,
And a proud remembering
Poppy flower.

Each year, we will
always remember,
And honour the noble
in November,
The fallen will forever
have our respect,
Every one of them:
For lest we forget.

Geoff Smith, poet and author

Geoff Smith

Geoff is a retired Anglican Priest who is now a writer. He has published a poetry anthology The Poem Must be Spoken, biographical fiction Serafina inspired by the life of Josephine Butler, novel Holy Disorder, and his new novel The Gorton Gospel will be published by Foreshore Publishing.

Geoff's latest project is writing a four line poem every day and posting them on social media.
These poems have been characterised as 'Cumbrian Haiku' and a selection is given here.
See Geoff's blog: www.myreversingmirror.blogspot.com

Cumbrian Haiku

Reaching towards far distant horizons
Where possibility comes with each turn
Heading homewards where loved ones
Are patiently awaiting our return

Climbing high peaks into rain cloud
This sense of life's burdensome weight
Hoping to somehow become the change
Trying to share the joy of love over hate

Planning the future hoping only
For the best. Tracking meteor showers
In night skies. Following the deer
Across the fell. Telling the hours

High pressure, feeling the pressure
Trying to remain relaxed despite
The pressure. Hoping for change
Preferring flight to fight

Welcoming strangers brings blessings
On the future becoming of our community
Memories of the past echoing faintly
As we endeavour to seize this opportunity

Memories of those who have been loved
Lighting candles, each flame
A precious memory before God
Rising as prayer, recalling their names

Sharing good news on the airwaves
Celebrating friendship's values
Hoping for a world that can change
Discovering the marvellous

In a world of painful division
Let's fly the flags of peace unfurled
Raise your hand in salute
Celebrate the unity of our world

Seeking to improve the sound track
Of life, searching the record shops
Revolution was too slow at 33 1/3
45s were always Top of the Pops

Being physically alone, feeling
Space around me more quietly
Embodying this experience of being
I exist in the air differently.

On a warm evening, as stars shone
Brightly, conversation intensified
Neighbours shared a sociable evening
So community was realised

In the silence of the chapel
Peace is shared, the unending
Peace of those who practice
The eternal gift of soul friending

The road ahead is closed, we are diverted
Turning left is often better so left we turn
Heading towards the possibility of spending
More than we could ever earn

Moving slowly towards growth
Climbing the ladders, avoiding snakes
Making progress in theory means
Doing in practice whatever it takes

Walking the shoreline barefoot
Catching the warm oceans tide lift
Thinking of the need for change and rest
Recognising the need for another shift

Circling the earth the sun rises
And sets on desert and forest canopy
Transforming darkness to light
Illuminating this world's gracious panoply

Pizza, Curry, kebab the foods
Of old England, enjoying the flavours
Of our immigrant culture as we eat
We welcome the stranger whose food we savour

A day of changes as each cross
Rearranges the politics of love and hate
Democratic responsibility is burdensome
So cast that vote, carry the weight

Mackerel skies shining red
Sun reflecting from Solway
Esk and Eden waters make borders
Salmon choose the separate way

I was seeking a future only to find
That it had passed before I could
Feel the wind, appreciate sunshine
Watch deer's stillness in the wood

From dusk to dawn a changing
World turns on its axis in pain
As wars and rumours of wars spread
The earth is crying for peace again

Waking to a day of promises
Fingers crossed hoping they're true
Promises I've made to myself and others
Promises I hope I don't rue

In the dear heart of loneliness
Struggling for survival
Knowing that with each secret shared
We're closer to revival

Kat van Hookens, poet and artist

Kat van Hookens

Kat van Hookens is one of five children born and raised on a small Somerset farm that nestles between the Quantock Hills and Exmoor. Helping out on the farm from an early age developed her deep love for the countryside which reflects in many of her poems. She credits her ability as a poet and artist to the sheer beauty of those surroundings and to her English teacher mum's encouragement and enthusiasm for all things natural.

Her first job on leaving college was as a laboratory assistant in a sedimentation unit where she studied geology and mineralogy. After that she eventually became chief technician in various schools, and also qualified to teach adult art. In 1990 she and her husband moved to France where they lived for fifteen years absorbing the culture and learning a second language. Whilst there she met and learned from several gifted artists, started a plein air painting group, and won several prizes for her artwork. She has also written a few poems in French.

Writing and painting now mean more than ever to her, and she relishes the fact that her work can bring pleasure to other folk…

Mums Only!

Why are Mums so wonderful? Have you ever stopped to
 think?
They're the only people smart enough to clean the kitchen
 sink.
To wash away the tide mark of goo and grease and grime,
Feed the dog, de-flea the cat and iron at the same time.
Only Mums it seems are able to pick towels up off the floor,
Take the soap out of the water, hang robes upon the door.
Only Mum's dexterity lets her replace a spent loo roll,
Put the lid back on the toothpaste and brush the toilet bowl,
Pick up dirty undies and turn socks the right way in,
Take tissues out of pockets hiding in the linen bin.
The gang stares in amazement as Mum hangs out the
 clothes,
Props up abandoned cycles and coils the garden hose.
Incredibly our Mums have learnt to hang coats upon coat
 hooks,
To refold crumpled newspapers and return the library
 books.
They even have the know-how to quietly shut a door,
Stand wellie boots against the wall and pick mud up off the
 floor.
Again it's Mum who's got the brains to shake the tablecloth,
Put the lid back on the jam and turn the telly off.
Without our Mums we'd surely be in misery and mess,
Kids and Dads, well they're okay, but Mums, they are the
 best.

... the bottom meadows at Nethercott were a wonderful playground for all of us al year round, but especially so on the long hot summer days. It was such a treat to trek down the hill, under the railway arch and into the long, grassy meadow with mumma, and take our swimming gear and a picnic. We spend the time running in and out of the stream. We would build camps under the trees, and dam the little river to make deep pools to play in. Dear mumma would help us make a campfire, she would make tea by boiling water in an old baked bean can and cook sausages to crispy blackness. The little steam train ran along the top of the slope, and all us kids would race up to the line a wave to the folks, and always they, and the engine driver would wave back, wonderful magical times...

Artwork from 'A Farming Journal: The Way It Used To Be'
by Kat van Hookens

The Repugnant Potion

Works better than whisky and a plethora of pills,
This repugnant infusion will cure all yer ills.
Toe nails 'n' pig tails and putrified swedes,
Dog dribble n toad's warts n decayed centipedes.
Hard wax from bats ears n festering mould,
Mixed with pee from a cow pat before it's gone cold.
All ground up on a millstone smeared with stinky dead
 crow,
Then stewed in a sheep's skull till it emits a green glow.
Then add a big handful of boiled macaroni,
This recipe, well, 'tis a load of baloney!

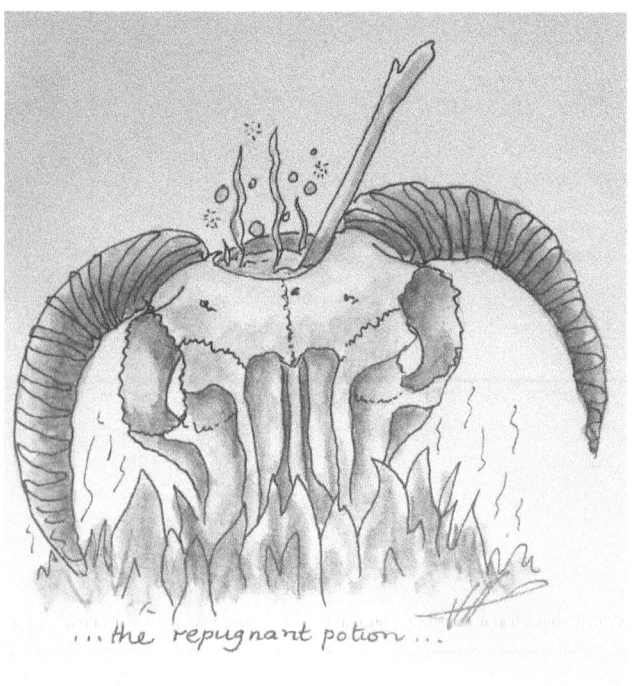

... the repugnant potion ...

Who'll weep for the trees?

How I envy your gift of flight,
light as a feather you rest in my hands,
nest in my arms.
You'll weep for me I know
as I wait on death row.
Below my canopy I carry the mark,
the graffiti of progress,
the sign of the white cross sprayed rudely on my bark.

I've sheltered them from summer showers,
given them flowers rich with heady perfume,
each enchanted bloom a joy to behold.
For autumn I laid carpets of red and gold,
gave them cause to dance, the young and the old.
The finest fruits I've yielded,
the deal did not consider me, year after year
there was no fee.

I hear progress coming.

My sisters curtsey their exit one
by one, ever graceful,
nowhere to hide, no way to run.
My crime remains uncertain as
the final curtain falls.
Who'll weep for me?
Who'll weep for the trees?

You gotta love a lolly

I'm on hols with me sister in a small town in South Devon,
Her gardens full of bees and flowers a proper little heaven,
'Tis on the edge of Dartmoor and very near the coast.
She's welcoming and homely, a hostess with the most.

Close by's a tiny hamlet that nestles by the sea,
Where lives one of me heart throbs, a real celebrity.
A dashing handsome film star, Bill 'the hunk' Burkote.
When I see him on the telly, he really floats me boat.

Well, one day whilst walking to the beach, the sun was
  mighty hot,
I thought I'd pop into a cafe to check out what they'd got,
I saw a sign for lollies, a treat of fruity ice.
'Twas a long time since I'd had one so I thought 'twould be
  nice.

The cafe looked deserted but the door was open wide,
So I tottered up the wooden steps and then I went inside.
I sorted out me money and headed for the till.
And there seated at a table was hunky brown eyed Bill.

I stopped and gawped and stared at him, he smiled and said
  hello,
I mumbled something in return, confused and all aglow.
I stumbled to the counter, me heart banging in me chest,
And in that fruity icy lolly I'd completely lost interest.

But somehow I got me lolly, and fumbled with me purse,
As my state of dumb confusion went from bad to worse.

I turned and peeked at Billy, all beefy in his vest,
Then teetered past my heart throb, puffing out me chest.

I swooned out from the cafe then realised me blunder,
I needed to go back again, would Bill spot my goof I
 wonder?
And think this crazy woman has shuffled off her trolly?
I had me change hot in me hand but I'd forgot me lolly.

Well I really need that lolly now, I'm baking hot and
 flustered,
So I walk back in and smile at Bill, who still looks hot as
 mustard.
He says with some amusement whist giving me a grin,
'You've got yer money in yer hand and it's yer purse yer
 lolly's in."

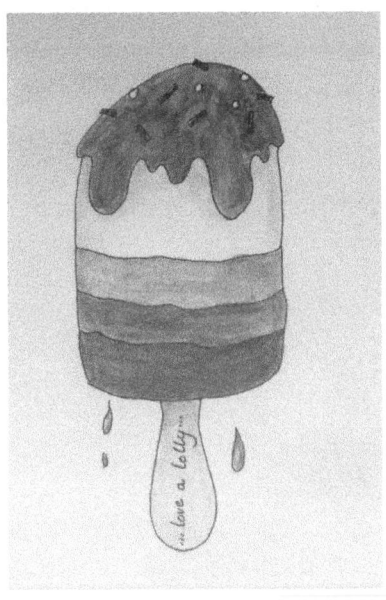

Mud's Thicker than Blood

Keep on churning out the poison, keep on chucking out the
 waste,
Don't stop stripping global assets, overdosing on bad taste.
Revel in the avarice, glory in the greed,
Wallow in excuses, encourage over breed.
Burn up all the forests, GM a hyper bug,
Gorge on all creation. Deaf and blind and smug.
Tarnish all the magic, stuff the kids with pap,
Turn our gifts to garbage. Fill the oceans up with crap.
Soon there'll be no birds to chorus, no skies of crystal blue,
Dawn won't bother coming when the sunbeams can't get
 through.
Have we used up all our chances, thrown away the key?
Is the cold dark morning coming when the Earth will be set
 free?
Free of all our want and greed, free from daily grind,
Free from pomp and piety, free of all mankind.
Denying truth up to the end, the final selfish flood,
Where blood's thicker than water, but not as thick as mud.

Stuart Turner, poet and singer

Stuart Turner

Stuart Turner was born on 7th May 1942 in Newcastle and spent his childhood in Consett, a steel town in County Durham (the Steel Works closed in 1980). He belongs very much to the Christian family and the upholding of Christian traditions. He attended Annfield Plain Secondary Modern School and was introduced to Literature, in particular, by his Headmaster, who was a brilliant man with the iconic name of W.E.Gladstone.

He started writing poetry in1962 after he joined the Royal Air Force and concentrated more specifically on this after the millennium in 2000 when he had more time after raising a family. He has engaged in both verse and prose, and his writing usually focuses on a mixture of nature and human interaction.

Urban Observations, June 2024

The sun shone with that
Brassy glare piercing
Clouds high above.

The countryside possessed
A not quite faded look
Criss-crossed by swallows.

Nearer half a dozen
Juvenile seagulls chased a gaggle
Of schoolboys leaving foody detritus.

Nearer still the urgent
Noise of a lawnmower, electric
Whirring frantically.

Eager to finish its task
Before threatening nimbus clouds
Unleashed their rain within.

An omnibus wheezed past
Leaving grey clouds and carcinogens
In its passing - like a ship's wake

But noxious and deadly
Not merely salty bubbles
And a few hopeful gulls.

A butterfly, an orange tip
Fluttered and poked its probiscus
Nose and front legs into a petunia.

Around the corner a noisy
Gang of crows were chasing a
Starling dragging a worm in its beak.

A cold breeze hardly more than a zephyr
Sprang up, clouds momentarily hid the sun
And it looked and felt more like autumn.

Then I noticed close by a wall
A small cat dabbing at
Something small and green.

It was my tiny common green lizard!
I jumped up and with the aid
Of my stick, held off the cat

Until 'Lizzie' as I had christened her
Found a crack in which to hide
And stay until dark then came up.

Later towards quickening twilight
I had finished watering my plants
When I sensed rather than observed

A dark form slinking around
The yard of the Indian takeaway -
'Reynard', my urban foxy rascal.

But fled as a noisy man and
Woman booled around the corner
And fox took to his heels.

I could hear pigeons quietly muttering
Something flashed by my head
I took it to be a bat.

Lights were going out
Minor rustlings came on the
Almost still air, then - silence.

I stood a few seconds, glanced
At the starry sky, fainter in
The glow of street lamps.

Then went inside, ready
For a mug of tea, maybe
A dram then sleep, day done.

To The Hills

I must go back to the hills again
To the quiet hills and the sky
To the moors and heather uplands
Where the curlew pipes his lonely cry.

Where the winds blow soft or fierce
And the lek of the grouse is heard
Where the shadows creep to darkness
And the bleat of a sheep is heard.

I must go back where the air is clear
And the white clouds pattern the sky
Where the cotton-grass nods its fluffy head
And the soft breeze emits a sigh.

Or on dark dark days when the autumn moans
And the wild geese honk to warmer climes
And moss shrivels on the cold north wall
Where the shepherd yearns for better times.

I must go back to the hills again

Suli's Dream

Suli wiped his brow.
Despite winter, he was hot
And perspiring.
It was not the sweat however
Of his own company, of central area -
It was the sweat of industrial working
Of biscuit making, his employers
Were indulgent, kind
He had worked hard to learn
Production techniques.

There had been training, but
His simple (*not* stupid)
Simple as in uncluttered mind
And his manual dexterity were
Beyond teaching.
He was what he was.

The management didn't sack him
Throw him out
He was not discarded, but given
A new challenge.
They sent him to P Plant
Where a change of working conditions
Allowed him and others to
Complete essential tasks but at a slower rate.

And Suli thrived; he might not be fast at packing
But at a pace that suited him, he came
Into his own

He was diligent, hardworking and resourceful
He was praised, people liked him
He helped his supervisor frequently
Now he whistled or sang.

He was happy.
He was making a life for himself, and his family
He had three children
All took after him.
In this new home
They were thriving.
Back home his mother would be so proud
The village would be proud.

One day, maybe not too long away
He would become a supervisor
And wear the yellow jacket.
He cleaned up and bent to his labours.
'One day' he muttered under his breath.
'One day' he grinned his gap-tooth grin.
'Yeah, one day.'

Talkin', Walkin'

'Ooh! Ye bugger'
'Ya aal reet, Tom?'
'Aye, just a thumb brayed again!'

Cobblers last on back door
step, Grandad making hand-cut
leather to complete jobs.

Pitman, horsekeeper that did
Not quite provide enough money
To keep family with extras.

His doorstep workshop was
Opposite a funeral director's.
They had many laughs.

He knew by the weather
By sound, by touch
'There's the geese away'
He would announce.
'Autumn roond the corner.'

He would sing or whistle
Old World War One tunes
Then proclaim

'Aye, that's anither pair
Mended, 9s 6d in the
Pot, eh.'

He lit his nose warmer
Leaned against the door-post
And muttered 'aye, aye.'

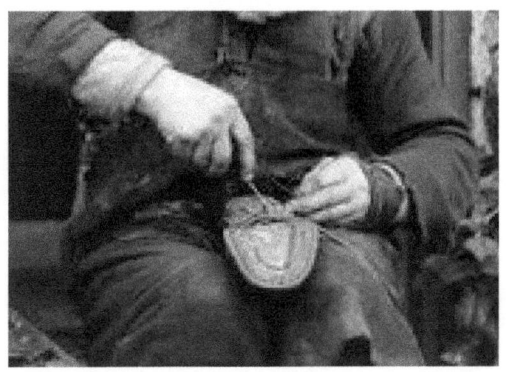

Money saving

In the yard outside
My father
With carbide lumps
On a stool
Making small lumps
From large ones.
Then pouring the
Smaller bits into
An old blue
Sugar bag
Labelled 'Carbide'.
Ready for pit use,
He sniffs and
Nods his head.

Katie Evans, poet

Katie Evans

Although technically not a Brampton resident, I am now a welcomed member of the Brampton Poets Group. I am a new member who is deeply appreciative of the opportunity to be able to listen and to learn from the works of some highly skilled poet-smiths. Having so far spent a life of travel and of education in other cultures, it is an honour to learn of a culture that I have come from, and it is an equal privilege to have a literary home to return to in the shape of this group's meeting room. Outside of my fellow Brampton Poets, I find inspiration from people who stand out for their individual attributes as well as collective identities that shine.

The poems I have chosen for my first contribution to the Brampton Poets reflect these influences, as well as the landscapes that I have fallen in love with on my travels. Two poems may require a little information. *Altiplà, Sant Jordi* is a poem from my journeys. The poem is simply set, stood on a plateau in the heart of Catalonia, looking out over a vast semi-arid horizon of little agricultural settlements draped in sunset. *Word Witch* is a sentimental poem, about a poet with power in their words, like a conjurer with their spells. A special thank you goes to the readers of this anthology. Thank you for your support.

County man

man of the dawn man of the street man of the tram man of
the rock man of the bleak man of the yellow man of the fur-
nace man of the pick man of the pony man of the gas man
of the cough man of the lung man of the bowed man of the
mire man of the valley man of the heath man of the cobble
man of the brick man of the wall man of the yard man of the
door man of the living room man of the chair man of the
table man of the cup man of the tea man of the plate man of
the slice man of the meat man of the cloth man of the shirt
man of the cotton man of the baby man of the cry man of
discipline man of upstairs man of the lamp man of short
nights man of sleep

Altiplà, San Elordi

*'Altiplà' in Catalan means plateau, as in the geographical
formation. 'Sant Jordi' is the Catalan name for Saint
George, the patron saint of Catalonia.*

The sun himself was on fire,
hurtling towards Earth
and yet the sun couldn't touch her.

The sphere dissolved
under the line of land in the horizon.
It was like sending your son, great general,
To sleep.

She, Earth
fell into a violet mist.
The cypress trees stood their vigil; sombre green
in the peach blue.

Bee-hum of streets,
white as a hospital.
Altiplà, halcyon.

Word witch

Word witch. You are a witch with spells
to curse & to praise.
You, gentle soul
Urbica urbica
You, chest of courage when you say
wily words up into the ether.

It should have been you
who crossed the Rubicon.
Eyes kind as doves.
Your pen drips with honey or with Aqua Tafona,
Lady of the snakes.

You are not a victrix, you are a reclaimer.
You, who reclaims the wrongs
of sullen sods
and scarpered angels' wings torn off;
Cast a spell, you seam those wings back on

You, whose smile connotes warm wine by the fire,
whose medallion round her neck
connotes Boudica on the rise.

You are the arbiter of poison
but you are not a poisoner
Urbica urbica
Embracer of mild nights
and soft songs,
Play on

Notes:

1. *'urbica' derives from the Latin name for the Western house martin, 'delichon urbica'.*

2. *'Aqua Tafona' was the potion sold by the professional poisoner Giulia Tafona in a ring of six Roman poisoners in the 17th century. The potion was sold to wives of abusive men who, because of Roman laws at the time, could not divorce their husbands, and thus turned to conspire their husbands' untimely deaths.*

3. *'victrix' in Latin means female victor.*

Chronology of Rona

unmotared stone

Hraun-oy Ron oy
Rónaigh an Daimh
Saint Ronan

grave markers in Scots
hermits. monks

rats. blackened grains

to Rona to Rona.
swells on the rock

remains of fire. pots of flesh. bird flesh. bones

The King of Rona left his isolation
sheep drown graze wonder sleep

sail. shot

automated lighthouse
unmotared stone

Stephen Palmer

Stephen was born in Carlisle and attended schools there before going to St John's College, York where he qualified to be a teacher, drank a lot of beer and played rugby. He returned to Cumbria where he taught in Primary Schools and raised a family with his wife, Ray, at Warwick on Eden for 40 years after a few years in Longtown. He has always lived near to a river until they moved to Cumwhitton where they are now close to a little beck.

As well as being a teacher he has also been a youth worker and a magistrate, latterly in the Family Courts.

Although raised in Harraby he has a close affinity to the countryside and feels most at ease walking, birdwatching, fishing and gardening.

Stephen has always been an avid reader and enjoys all sorts of writing and these are a few of his poems.

Haiku Calendar

Glancing back to dark
staring far into mystery
no pausing time now

Deep in soaking leaves
life goes on hardly moving
waiting better days

Goldfinch in stark hedge
face rouged by crucifixion
searching for lost fruits

Raining on flowers
softening warmth gaining ground
green spears to alert

Scattered May blossom
hazing over   white capped trees
crows crop sparrow chicks

Warm winds and long days
grass to laze and love upon
disappointing times

Corner of the year
seaside heatwaves shimmering
a smeared horizon

Above our rooflines
swifts describe highest markings
before being gone

Autumn failing now
shortening winter days soon
spring a distant dream

Fieldfares snatch berries
flash outwards baring branches
leaving sad quiet

Black etched onto grey
leaves on fire then earth bound soil
before rain resumes

Cold ponds still living
motionless as tin platters
soon to be harder

Carol

A schoolgirl who watched vapour trails and flak,
heard merlin engines above Northumbrian dunes
when black crossed shapes flocked from the east.
Carol flew to far away places to nurse and stayed,
long enough to meet an admiralty-something-or-other
who she followed round his postings for years
until they tired of living from suitcases and landed back.

Carol and her chap settled in here by the church,
happy with each other,   with their horses and dogs
but without children   and when she was without him
after years together, she was lost but chose to stay
and find another way, with pictures and antiques ,
with an empty stable, an empty kennel
and an empty bed. But oh, the birds and beasts
in her garden, in her shed and among the tangled shrubs.

Carol fastened back her stable door again last year
as always for swallows returning to fly in, fly out ,
fly in and out until   more flew out than in.
Martins under her house eaves, five pairs there,
first to come and then leave before the last fall.
Hirundines in and out and around her pleasure,
tracery laced her sky, their sky, striated in every way.
Carol knew how many broods they had in all,
They crowded the wires   in family flights and waited.

Carol slipped once,   then slipped again and faded,
slipping in and out and in and out
and was gone by August last year

before the leaving the birds here,
leaving someone else to close the stable door.
The man who moved in said he wouldn't
do that anymore because of the mess.

Dementia

Across the back field J. appeared, waving ,
calling his dog and my name,
laughing at his cavorting collie,
clear as the day,   crisply focussed
before he was gone
into a dip in the soft ground.

When I saw him again he'd faded more,
through the slowly drifting billows of mist .
I thought it was him but vaguely ,like a bent stick,
then he was lost again and there was a fog
between us, although his arm lifted hesitantly.

Later still I could just glimpse his dog
scraping the ground behind and around it before
the light changed , dimmed down, softly edged
and maybe a bare tree stood
with a branch pointing upwards.

Then again maybe   a man, maybe Jay,
then he'd gone again and the dog turned,
as dogs do before sleep,   again and again,
but with his head back, silently howling ,
sniffing the cold ground, searching , searching.

Lastly a tree again briefly
but no clearer although with two branches up.
Then fallen and vaguely recognisable,
a man I didn't know
asleep
covered by mist.

Our window cleaner

Our window cleaner has a big smiling face
and big brown arms with big muscles
in places where I don't have muscles.

He calls me 'sir' because I'm old
despite my protests   he just smiles and smiles
whether it's raining   or I've forgotten to pay him.

He smiles about fishing at home
In Africa where he has his   aged mother.
The great big silver snoek eaten
from the surf sizzling on   the beach braai
above tideline and scattered wrack
how he smiles about those big silver fish.

He smiled today about the world cup
so   because he has big muscles
I asked If he'd played rugby and he smiled
he'd played for big clubs as a younger man
all over the place against some great players.

Smiling he told me how he'd played against
Maro Itoje   England's biggest and best
how they'd a tussled a bit after a tackle.
Our window cleaner smiled even more
about his yellow card for 'slapping' Itoje.

Our window cleaner's a big boy
'but that Maro' he smiled, ' is a big big boy .'
They'd laughed later with beers in the clubhouse

said our big window cleaner
giving me his biggest smile
and then cleaned our windows.

*Geoff Smith, Stephen and Ray Palmer, Phil Hewitson and
Baxter, at the 'Pop-up' Bookshop in Alex Boathouse
Talkin Tarn, August 2024*

Grassland

Old Mary died at lambing time
he said in the street
as the forage harvesters and silage trucks
roared deafeningly near us
through blued diesel fumes
streamed rock rap   reggae
tight into the ears of boy drivers
waving like contractor charioteers
without a care for air or nature
or even lambs it seems.

They worship at the altar of grass
four cuts of it and more a year
only one variety of it
one close cut   every month of it
from April nesting time to the fall
those mono-cultured fields
green like the fivers they create
all for mega-machines and dairy cattle.

Mounds and heaps and plastic rolls of it
sweet smelling cow-cud   food
making factory milk and cheeses
tight belts   fat bottoms
and cardiac diseases
double cream for double chins
at the cost of lapwings and curlews
wiped out by lush grass
and the wealth its cutting brings
for the grandsons of old Mary.
Who died at lambing time.

Jean Taylor, poet

Jean Taylor

Jean has lived in Cumbria for thirty years and in Brampton for six years.

She was born in Liverpool in 1932 and joined Martins Bank in 1948.

In 1954 Jean joined the Wrens and worked at the Admiralty Building in London. Having left the Wrens to get married Jean had four children and worked alongside her husband running their own dairy business in Liverpool until they both retired at 61 and moved to Cumbria.

Ken 99 Ice Cream Party.

I have a famous brother-in-law
He was a navigator in the war.
Ken found war was not his dream
So he made the locals fresh ice cream.

He found this task quite a breeze,
Therefore had in mind food to freeze.
A shrewd investment then was made,
Deserving of an accolade.

Everfresh was the company name,
Which gave Malpas quite some fame
And although Ken always liked a flutter,
The frozen food was his bread and butter.

With local people's helping hand
Ken made Everfresh a well-known brand
Companies came and made him offers
Helping swell Ken's pension coffers

Parties at Malpas were fun every year,
laughter and dancing with never a tear.
Friends old and new enjoying the night
With Ken as ever witty and bright.

So we all look forward to a party next year,
when Ken is 100 and we clap and cheer.
We hope good King Charles will also appear
And bring Ken's birthday card for his special year.

Now we toast our Ken on this special day
So let's raise our glasses…. Hip, Hip, Hooray!

WRNS

After seven years in the Bank
in need of more adventure
I joined the Wrens

Navy skirt, white blouse and tie
jacket, cap and neatness
I looked the part

I was 22, it was after the War
and I trained in Signals
in Hampshire

The training camp was HMS
Mercury and I remember
the glorious weather

Six months later I was ready and
soon moved to the Admiralty
working below ground

in Churchill's secret Cabinet Offices
typing telephoned messages
then sending them on

keeping the Navy engine running
a weather report every week
to the entire fleet

Good Memories; meeting the Queen Mum
Princess Margaret and Kenneth More
Oh, My goodness!

So many things I did in just two years
Before I left to get married
                    And the adventure continued…

Blue

At 7 in 1939
My father took me to my first match
The last at Goodison before the War.
A Police Sergeant he knew Dixie Dean
whose record for headed goals
has never been beaten.

My husband's Dad was from Liverpool
His Mother was from Cumbria
Her family were expert in cows and Dairy
and we became the fifth generation
in the family business.

My Mother was a seamstress in Bold Street
making dresses for actresses
but she had to give it up
when she got married.
That was how it was then.

Mum made our clothes and baked
Dad worked and grew food
in the garden and allotment.
It was not always easy but
we did alright.

Dale Farm Dairy, that later supplied
milk to us, had their own private box
at Goodison Park so we enjoyed
all the times we went there, watching
Everton as VIPs

Because, you know, it's so true
that once you're a Blue
you're always a Blue…

Roots

If you ask me where I'm from
I'll tell you that's an easy one
It's Liverpool!

There till I was 61
Liver Birds, St George's Hall
What a city

A sense of humour all our own
the Docks, the Mersey Beat
A lively place

I'm a Blue - that's Everton
football's in my genes and blood
and Liverpool's in my heart…

Philip Brown

Born in 1940, I grew up in Stretford, Manchester, and was educated at Manchester Grammar School and Oriel College, Oxford, where I read Chemistry and then did a DPhil in organic chemistry. I married Helen in 1963 and then, with her and our six week old daughter, spent two years carrying out research at the University of California at Berkeley and another two at the University of Adelaide, South Australia, where our first son was born.

I then took up a lectureship at Newcastle University, our second son appearing shortly afterwards. I stayed at Newcastle until we both retired and moved to our small holding below Spadeadam.

In earlier years my main interests were piano playing, classical music, choral singing, and mountaineering, the latter becoming hill walking and scrambling. I took up composing music more seriously when I was given a Sibelius package for my 60th birthday but only recently turned to writing poetry for its own sake rather than as an adjunct to music.

In Vain I Search Your Face

A response to several madrigals concerned with unrequited love.
In no way autobiographical.

In vain I search your face
  for signs of love reciprocal of mine for you.
No warmth lies in your greeting smile,
  no crease attends your eyes
   wherein the only feelings shown
  are but reflections of my own.
Your lips remain unparted
  yet still do they beguile
   whilst my heart, my heart is piercèd through
  as hope within me dies.

  Such coldness now dictates
I wait, while slow Time turns
  and by its passing
my heart itself outburns
  and the hurt abates.

Here, Just Here

Here, just here we lay,
 sheltered by this heaven-scent gorse
  that sanctioned so sweet a kiss,
 and then one more, and more,
  and oh yet more,
 one for every flower.

Side by side we gazed
  beyond the serenading lark,
    beyond the silver sliver of a day-time moon,
  beyond the blue itself
    and saw those spheres
  that had, since time began,
   ground out their cycles,
  those epic cycles,
    just so that our stars
  aligned – precisely – so.

And for each the other was the one,
  for each the other was the one.

The Longer Way

We took the longer way,
  ostensibly to discuss
   the Bergman film that we'd just seen
   played out upon the silver screen,
    but really to prolong the parting day.

There came a gentle, floating rain
  that dampened locks and soon was gone
   but left a freshness in the air
   that promised new beginnings
    – if only one but dare.

Hands touched and fingers met
  then held more tightly still
   to start a warming glow
  that slowly spread to every part
until, in my bewildered heart,
   it lit a fire that burns bright yet.

Andromeda

This fancy took root after I read that Andromeda, our neighbouring and much larger, galaxy is set to engulf the Milky Way in due cosmological time.

And when Andromeda's course is run,
  if not well before – what then?
A Perseus to save the day
  and keep intact our Milky Way?
A caring, benign hand
  to gently guide this Earth
   through unimaginably rough seas
  to calmer waters where a gentle breeze
  will lead us to a great rebirth
on some more lush, congenial strand?

Already we can clearly see
  what havoc just one mere degree
   can wreak upon our world and cause
  such harm, equal to that of all our wars.
Dark Erebus would then seem
  as Paradise itself when forces so extreme
   pursue their cold, unyielding will
  and all life limps and whimpers towards – nil.

Will even traces of our Sun exist,
  let alone those of our small sphere?
Will any memories of Earth persist
or will they fade and then just – disappear?

The loves and hates in all men's hearts,
   the good they mostly try to do,
man's high achievements in the sciences and arts
  and yes, the monstrous acts of evil too,
will they live after us or be forever lost
   in some deep, near-zero permafrost?

Now, back within our present time,
   it's sometimes said that walls of stone can keep alive
  all memories of our sojourns here:
   that in some strange and unknown way
  even those from long ago can still adhere.
We cannot say what laws they might obey
   but after action so sublime
  could these faint ghosts, even stone itself, survive?

And yet – it's maybe of some comfort now to think
  the universe will keep a link,
  a faithful copy made in quantum mode
   and held in interlocking rings
  of multiple, entangled strings
   within an umpteen-dimensioned QR code,
  then tunnelled to a wave-mechanic node
   and there recorded on a parallel, alternate brane.
  Don't ask - I can't explain.

For, even if entombed, with no way back,
  in some black hole, a cul-de-sac,
  it's now believed
  that data *can* still be retrieved
  from such an all-engulfing site
 of gross, destructive appetite.

So code could be unravelled in a future lab
   and then deciphered by an aeonologist from – the Crab?
  who might contemplate in awe
   at what, for Earth will be it's now
 with all that we might then endow,
  but will be, for them, their well before.

But put aside such idle fancies,
   and don't have fears
   about such intellectual romances:
  let's enjoy our here and now.

If all the world's a play upon a stage
   then we've not reached the final page,
   so shed no tears,
  it's not yet time for Earth to take its final bow.
The ending when it finally occurs
  won't happen for four billion years.

Winter's Wood

In Winter's Wood I saw more beauty
  than in many a scented summer scene.
    Long had I thought, on blind men's instruction,
     that all was black and barren,
    a formless montage of extremes of grey
save when heightened by contrasting traceries of fern-like frost
or doubled into glory by limpid garlands of suspended snow
             poised
                 for
                   further
                       flight.

The dawning broke, a halcyon day.
  The buffet-wind of night
    was swept away
     in a broad expanse of blush-edged blue
      and rivers sang beneath their ice
     whilst every slanting ray
    of warm-felt morning light
   drew colour of such subtle hue
  from each supporting tree
asleep beneath the arching canopy.

Tight-furled beech buds, tan, and purpled birch,
  Their peeling bark a parchment pale
    whilst old, grey ash, lichen-lifted to a glacial sage
    bore buds as black as the bright-billed ouzel
     side-swooping from its singing perch
      through the stand of straight limbed hazel
     whose every old-gold tail
    trembled without pause
   attempting to engage
their unmoved scarlet paramours.

A yew, dark as the carpet of white-patterned moss
    and marking still its ancient edge,
        guarded now the buff, dried sedge
          whilst, upward thrusting in their turn,
          the pastel fronds of fledgling fern
        still mourned, heads bowed, the loss yet raw,
their fallen forbears, fawn, on the forest floor.

While ever thankful for such gifts,
  What other pleasures have I missed,
being, by some other muse, as yet, un-kissed?

Mary Thornton, poet

Mary Thornton

Mary worked in London in the seventies as a nurse, in Westminster, and spent an enjoyable year following that, in the charcuterie at Harrods, which was great fun. After this, she studied teaching at Newcastle Poly, and in 1983 moved, with her family to Brampton, where she ran an antique shop, and a market stall, (quite incompetently she wishes to add!) Finally, she taught children with learning difficulties for fifteen years.

Mary enjoys painting, writing, and just being in this most beautiful part of our world.

Alphabet for geriatrics...

A is arthritic and anal retention
B is bad back causing complete abstention
C is for chest pains...cardiac dysfunction
   and circulation going up the junction
D is for a discogram of a declining spine
E is for eyesight, - can't read the top line.
G is for gastro-intestinal tract
   (a lot can go wrong with it, that's a fact!)
   and not to forget other possible glitches
H is high blood pressure,
I   for itches and stitches.
J   is for joints now failing to bend
K is for knee, refusing to mend
  and now for
Libido, I've put that away for a while
   who needs libido if no longer fertile!
M is for memory, what's that? –I forget
N is pinched nerve, stiff neck and neurosis
O is the onset of osteoparosis
P is prognosis, hopefully good
Q feeling queasy, more than I should.
R is for reflux, when breakfast returns
S back to sex, has to be relearned.
T is for time, very slow passing time
Ultimately (that's U) I'll be feeling just fine
V when a vein gets a nasty blood clot
Warfarin to take, kills the clot, rats, the lot.
X is for x-rays – hundreds of them
Y is for feeling young again – I hope – soon
   and now that I've come to the very last letter,

   just writing this has made me feel better
Z is for zest – not the orange peel type
   but sparkling with energy, zinging with life

Folding you in my heart.

*I was a bit worried about what I might be like after an op,
so I wrote a little ditty of thanks, and this is what it came out
like!! (adopting the style of Wm Spooner, who when sending
one of his students down from Oxford for time wasting said
'You have hissed my mystery lectures, you have tasted a
whole worm, and you will leave Oxford by the town drain'
or... You have missed my history lectures, you have wasted
a whole term etc...*

And now that I'm meeling on the fend
I'll be good, and not bist or twend
My wretched back is seeling fore
I must try not to boan and grore

Everyone's been so very good
I'll have to thank them,
I shearly rould.
So hank you thartily,
all my friends
and noctors and durses,
and pen we whart.
I'll remember you all fondly
Folding you in my heart.

A New Meaning for Provocative!!

I've had a dodgy vertebrae
It's gripped me in painful throes,
And knocked me down right to the ground
Whenever I blew my nose.

I'd shriek and howl and swear a lot,
It would only last a while.
My feet would go dead, my back go hot
But still, I managed to smile.
(*it was, however, a fixed rictus smile*)

So I went to see the surgeon Nick
In a city a far from home.
'I can fix it', said he, 'But it won't be quick'
'And I'll have to use some of your bone'.

'Now first I'll need look at some details
Like where most of the pain comes out.
So I'll stick you full of needles,
And I'll know when you start to shout!!'

SHOUT? not I, I'll not admit defeat,
Instead, I'm sure, my feelings I'll contain.
In went the needles, I gritted my teeth,
Trying hard not to show my pain.

'That wasn't so bad', then said I,
'I'm glad, that you now are done'.
'Not yet', said he with evil glee,
'There's one more yet to come'!

'Are you ready? Here goes',
And the needle went in,
With deadly and accurate aim.
and I shot up to the ceiling…
             …propelled by incredible pain!

'Is that your **normal** pain?' he inquired,
Through a swirling, foggy red, haze.
'Why not try it again'? I hissed through my teeth,
'Yes, that's normal, I get it most days'!!

Provocative now means a different thing
To what I thought it meant before
And it's nothing to do with sultry looks
That suggest just a little bit more.

It means huge great needles and truck loads of pain.
A sado-masochist's delight.
But having got this far I'll go the whole way
I'm going to finish this fight!!

Thoughts on Death

When a loved one dies,
we cling to the hope
that maybe they chose to wait,
to keep us company in their final moments.

Or, perhaps they chose to leave quietly,
with no fuss or tears,
to spare us the sadness.

Either way, we are left behind,
with the weight of grief and love,
wrestling with the mystery of death,
and some final line drawn under

But in the end, we must surrender,
to the truth that death is natural,
and that it brings both pain and peace.

A reminder to hold tight to those we love,
and to cherish the time too short,
we have together.

The Standing Stones

The stones stood tall
Solemn, silent in the gathering dusk.
The sky, previously busy with homebound birds
Now lay quiet and empty.
The sun slipped slowly down under the hills
Beneath the flaming red horizon
Leaving promises for a fine tomorrow.

And carefully, quietly, thoughtfully,
I stepped along the way
For maybe a mile or more,
Feeling the ancient ground
Through my sensitive soles,
As time melded

Past, present, and future,
Joined into a fleeting moment,
A mystery, a gift.
Walking on the edge of memory
Until the dark clothed me
And, torch in hand, I turned my face to home

David Simmons, poet

David Simmons

David Simmons was a keen sportsman, bicycler and backpacker until his body said enough. He now enjoys short walks to cafes, bus stops and railway stations. He likes to write poetry, including haiku, with observation, energy and movement. He loves Carlisle and its proximity to the natural landscape, especially the Eden Valley, where his mother was raised on a tiny hill farm.

Wiser than boundaries (after Tony Hendry)

Sumptuous Edenside
last tall summer gone,
no languid gait
you absorbed every blade,
rounding the ground
recalling them all, Sir Garry,
Sir Clive, Thommo with Lillee

of boundaries, wiser
perhaps a new pavilion,
where Roman horsemen bathe
and daydream of almond groves,
where steam and strigils cleanse,
where boasts in the Caldarium
tally with our Carvetian dead

here you'd generously
murder a ballad,
riff on Sally Wheatley,
eyes only for the Empress,
and Bridget's trowel easing
out the hypocaust tile, noting
sore knees and leaping heart.

We were all ears, you're talking
fractions of a second, no replay
for when it comes, hell,
some don't see it, maybe you,
Kookaburra, Dukes, glistening,
strikes temples hard, a bouncer,
like them Aussie quickies threw.

We coagulate, your kind,
recall that brave boy scout,
he'd say "bat on, show no fear."
Damn it Tony, we need *Fresh Air*,
poetry written in nature's way,
simple truths, honest through,
ever too the one to walk.

Illustration by Phil Hewitson of Romans
playing a match at Carlisle cricket ground
from 'Carlisle in Haiku Form' by David Simmons

Shoulders broader than borders

Honey, my honeybee
had asked, as if the clouds and
leaves could feel, take every drop of pain

our hesitation frayed, forlorn, forewarned
of harm, the inhospitable
stronger armed.

In unripe fields we saw rungless ladders
piled upon pyres, bloated snakes,
fingering feeding on dice,

bereft we tramped through sadness,
mobiles, moon bags blistering
with heft, our story.

Honey had dark smudges puddled on her face
a determination of extraordinary beauty
now more than half of me.

From fertile land we'd borne the loss of kith and kin
their soiled hands harried, hurried
by widespread interrogation.

I rewind her
bandages, scissor
time, pining for our country.

We gather twigs and
seek new songs, construct
a cage for friendships and love

in embers of
arguments and longings we flame
rehearsals, our intentions to return

under shared blankets
there are unfamiliar odours and
tones, fresh stains become ingrained

womb
and shoulders
grow broader than borders

sorry nan
the battery
almost gone.

Three haiku:

the neurodiverse
be who you are and rejoice
in what makes you you

kin-e-tic microbes
pumping up the volume for
gene pool rainbow dance

prism means potential
all abilities create
art gives therapy

Mason Goddard, poet and artist

Mason Goddard

Mason often writes his poems in the Brampton Poets meetings. Mason is an artist, makes jewellery and writes poems which one day he hopes to publish. Mason is also a member of the LGBTQIA+ community and supporter of local Pride events.

What a world

Even when you can't see us,
We exist
Even when they do not let us speak
We exist

I am human
I live
I breathe

I am a man
But I have to fight to be called a man
Fought to look like a man
And I will never be treated like a man

What a world we live in
Where there are laws against being human

What a world we live in
Where women cannot have conversations

What a world we live in
Where we must be dying to be helped

What a world we live in
Where people are murdered
For the colour of their skin
The town they were born
The love they feel
For their bodies
Their words
For their heart, their soul and their minds

They banned the books
They wrote the laws that killed
Their flags are red and so are their hands

Do I talk about the 1930s or the 2020s?

We will mourn tonight
But tomorrow?
Tomorrow we fight

Love me like a swan

Love me like a swan
With love eternal
Floating along like chiffon
With love that burns infernal

Love me like a god
With life intertwined
Like peas in a pod
Let us never be unkind

Love me like a sailor
Come and take sweet tea
As we watch the sky grow paler
Over the morning sea

Love me like a swan
Love me until we die
In the ground I die upon
Together we will lie

Ultraviolet

Hope is not fragile
Hope has blood under its nails, and
Streaming out its nose and pouring
Out of its mouth
Hope is ultraviolet
Hope is there when you cannot see it
Hope illuminates things you didn't even know
were there

Fear is a dull weapon
Fear is a sledgehammer to drywall
Fear has blood on its hands and
Crimes to answer for
Fear is the absence of hope
It is warm, it is bright, it burns inside you
It consumes all of the beautiful things
The things you never noticed were there
Fear is pain

Everything
Everywhere
Is on fire

Andromeda

And so we shall be wiped out
We shall be consumed
By a neighbouring galaxy
Our beloved Earth, wiped out

Andromeda, moving ever closer,
Crashing and swallowing
Drawn to this sphere of life
Death moving ever closer

The beach we walked down
Shall be walked upon no more
We shall take our last stroll
And watch the sun go down.

It shall never again grace the day.
The light cresting over the waves,
The sand burning our toes.
We shall never again grace the day.

The world is ending, it's you and me.
Let us lay with each other,
Let me gaze into your eyes
Some things are eternal, it's you and me.

June Moss-Luffrum, poet

Jane Moss-Luffrum

Former university teacher, based in Cumbria with my family
for more than forty years and involved with poetry writing,
groups, and performance for a long time, I have been
published in poetry magazines, anthologies, and online.
I enjoy any time spent with my three daughters, and two
granddaughters. My interests include art, photography, and
traditional music. My partner and I have always been keen
walkers and cyclists, making use of the opportunities at home
in Cumbria, and in our mountain bolt-hole in the Axarquia.

Theft

'A thief is someone in need.' (Khalil Gibran)

I stole a brick
from your giant Lego train.
I just found it in this tiny plane.
Strictly speaking, you put it in my bag
along with the other things
you gift and nick.

I've watched you with your treasure cache
openly purloined and relocated,
curated like marbles.
Usually stuff I've liberated -
slim packets of artificial sweetener,
sachets of needless
seedless jelly jam

You prize crumpled tissues,
my phone, my purse,
full of oily coins
everyone has touched
with unwashed hands.

Exchange is no robbery.
I didn't put the brick back.
It has a 2 on it. Your next birthday,
months away.

As you climb a step
and say 'um, do',
It feels like
that's enough for me.

I make myself know again,
in primary colours,
about emergency landings,
infant flotation devices,
where the oxygen drops down,
and sorting yourself out first.

I find that cord of ligament you like,
That radial socket in my elbow's inner crook
and knead it a little too hard.
It's sore, as if blood
has been taken.

I still feel your hand rest
and slip down my forearm.
Theft.
I pull down the tray in front of me.
A child has crayoned on it in red.

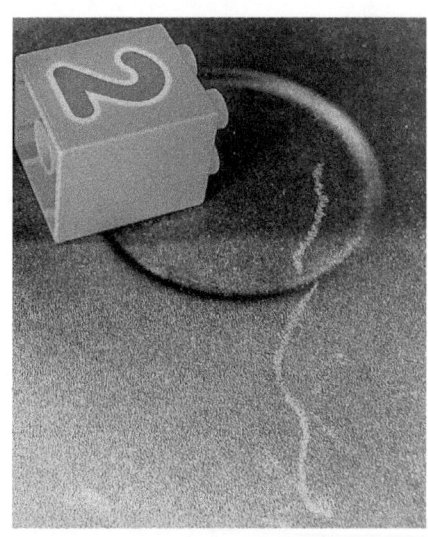

Achieving symmetry

The Angel of the North, cruciform
like Da Vinci's Vitruvian Man
out of his hamster wheel,
is designed to be seen
at creeping speed.
On the megalithic slag heap
of an old colliery hill
injected deep with mortar,
a rusted, rooted Gabriel
engulfed by trees.

The wings pointlessly
angled forward to welcome,
regular and symmetrical in shape,
simulacrum of bones,
an exoskeleton of serried ribs
directing the weather to its feet.

Morphed from ships containers,
bridges, boats,
coped in weathering steel.
No centre, just a corten bag of angles
celebrating nothing
with its bare airplane arms.
God's scarecrow
braced against the wind,
as if waiting for an embrace
it can't reciprocate.

We moved her in

We moved her in.
Her window is steeple high
and the view to the street
is steep.

In Paris once, I watched a man
walk calmly
from a window
as if leaving by the door.
You would have to squeeze through
sideways here
with clear intentions.

There are two screens
that hush past each other,
each sliding pane,
she informs me,
is safe glass.

On the top floor stairs the rail is low
and only probably not too low.
Each night she climbs the stairs
I will her to the wall side.

Somos Luz

She thinks they are animals
and now so do I.
The crystal hexagons
that become snowflakes,
engineered by gravity,
symmetry and electrostatics,
chemistry and magnetism.
In exact conditions
colourless, just light.

She thinks they are more.
Just four, she dropped her
cardboard crystal symbol
at the nativity,
freestyling among the stars
and farmyard animals.

She did it again solo at charades
at Christmas time,
when the theme was animals,
and everyone was hopping
or leaping or reaching for trees.
She just spun and spun and spiralled down

Made of star material,
unique like snowflakes,
we too have symmetry,
two of most things balanced in
and on a frame.
Bred perfect like snowflakes,
collecting unique patterns on our spokes,
as we spin and spin and spiral down.

The dog walk

It's rained all day so I do this short walk
I used to do last thing with my dogs.
It's autumn, past the equinox
but before they tamper with the clocks
and I'm not fully used to a short twilight.

Crisp beech nuts, unyielding
as uncollected children's bricks,
and wet beech leaves tough as plastic
line the way. I brush past
the sharp straw of dead plants,
their heads and seeds long gone.

The shivering ash still shimmering
in September, is passively sepia now.
My dogs are clean bones
at the bottom of the garden.
Sometimes I still feel a nose sharp
in the back of my knee
or hear the soft whine of despair
when my tears or questions
cannot be understood,
allayed or answered.

The path goes by a long farm,
put in part to other uses.
It used to be earth something
but it's air something now.
It still smells of beasts and raw wet meat.
There's a lighted barn for business,
an office in a byre. There's a long gap
in the hedge and a gate on posts
with no fence on either side.

A little further on they have neighbours,
in a bungalow with good views to Skiddaw,
a dormer with narrow doll house stairs
and no banister, somewhere unused good china,
and something someone made
with black velvet, strings and nails.
A front door of infrequent greetings,
and reluctant adolescent kin.
The smell of last illnesses.

At nearly night the view from the gate
is grained and I don't linger. I am myself
grey gauze and lightless.
Back past the farm, through a window
at some distance, a head rests
above the back of a settee.
The room flickering.
A man inside the house moves through
an unfinished knocked through archway.
He is slowly purposeful, and I find
I like the idea of it all very much.
He has thin dark hair, a check shirt and gilet,
he is shambling, but not stumbling.

The world smells of water. I see my house lights
dappling through the dark trees
and although I might live there alone,
I pretend I live there, alone.
I think of how I'd feel living in that house
in its little wood.
How it would be with no sound
nor greeting once the door
is bolted from inside.

Then I come through the wet grass,
and under the bowing trees
as the empty house emerges from them.
I think of how welcoming the lights
I've left on look, and how glad
anyone would be
to come there out of the night.

Phil Hewitson

Phil is a writer, poet, illustrator, graphic designer and film-maker born and raised in Carlisle. He makes films for Tolivar Productions, publishes books as Caldew Press, and hosts SpeakEasy spoken word open mic nights.

Papillon

Butterfly

My dear butterfly

You flash those coloured wings
Bat away those tumbling nerves

Swooped up in a fine net
You're a find, most cherished
Put inside a gold-lined box
Looked at through a glass

Did that lepidopterist pin you down
So you can't fly away
Small sharpened steel skewer
Pierces silk membrane
Those wings don't beat no more
Your lovely works of art
Wide open they are splayed

You don't fly
You don't flutter
You don't wave goodbye

My dear butterfly

Butterfly

Ever Present Presence

Oh you've got me in your pocket
You carry me around
I'm always there with you
I'm listening every time you make a sound

The places we can go
The things to you I'll show
Words, films and pictures
We've moved on from squiggly little scriptures

And voices at the end of the line
These days who has the time?
There are no wires, no ties that bind
Instant communication, whatever pops into your mind

That little mirror lights up like a Christmas tree
When you decide you want to talk to me
If the call is missed I'll have to ring you back
On that magic little device all shiny and black

Aurora Night

A storm breaks
ninety-three million miles from Earth
Ionised particles
cast off from the sun
strike the atmosphere
That invisible umbrella above a world,
the pale blue dot,
our fragile home
Unaware participant
in a galactic game of chance
Another round of Russian Roulette
Satellite communications fear blackout
Could the World Wide Web be cut off?
Modernisation hindered by ancient forces
A change from the threat of meteor impact
Crater created by megaton punch
Dust cloud did for dinosaurs
This cosmic dust cloud
reveals phantom beams of white
purple haze, shimmering pink and green
Each gas flares its own colour
Camera lens reveals detailed magic,
somewhat visible to the eye,
making Lyra Silvertongues of us all,
gazing up at Northern Lights,
enthralled by cosmic dust
…unless, of course, you missed it!
And end up gazing down,
at portable device,
as social media shows you
secondhand!

I was lucky enough to witness the aurora borealis (northern lights) on the night of Friday 10th May 2024 as they lit up the skies over much of the UK.
There was something magical about seeing them over my neighbourhood. Others were less fortunate and found social media flooded with photos.

My Beautiful Shadow

My beautiful shadow
The golden girl who follows me
And watches all the mistakes
I make

My beautiful shadow
Takes flight like Peter Pan
Journeys to Neverland
As I watch the stars shine

My beautiful shadow
Beams at me with eyes so bright
A story bubbling up inside
And she always keeps me right

My beautiful shadow
Is generous and kind
Likes the life she finds
In the sleepy town of words

My beautiful shadow
Is finding who she is again
Making endless friends
And living in each moment

My beautiful shadow
May leave now and then
But she comes back in the end
So far

My beautiful shadow

Walks a lonely path with me
Always makes me see
The world with eyes a-new

My beautiful shadow
Banishes away my cares
Each time into my soul she stares
I'll miss you when you're not there

My beautiful shadow

Parting Words

It seems that I
just can't say 'goodbye'
Sayin' 'cheers'
doesn't hide my fears
And 'I'll see you around'
doesn't mask the sound
of my heart
breaking every time we depart
Calling out 'adieu'
only makes me think of you
'Hasta la vista, baby'
Will there be a next time, and don't say maybe?
Is this our final 'Au revoir' my dear?
All my hopes reach their nadir
Show me the door
like you've done a million times before
Kick me out where I belong
don't worry I'll soon be gone
They say parting is such sweet sorrow
but I may well see you again tomorrow

Beyond Borders book launch, 1st December 2023

Reading in the Craft Room at Brampton Community Centre

David Simmons, Ena Hutchinson and Phil Hewitson plant trees

Dear Reader,

I hope you have had as much pleasure reading through this anthology as Brampton Poets have had producing this our sixth anthology.

The seed of an idea Gilbert & I had sown in late 2015, taken from Keswick's Words by the Water poetry morning we attended annually, to form a group to talk, discuss and enjoy reading poetry. We invited a friend, Stuart Turner, to join us, unaware then that he wrote poetry. We met in Brampton Community Centre behind the cafe kitchen. We began with croissants & marmalade, buying a jug of coffee from the cafe. The second month David Hurd & Laura Burnham joined us. Sadly they have both passed away. The following month John Langley had heard about us and came along, all bringing their own poetry to read.

Each month brought in new faces, Ruth Kershaw, David Bamford, then two Jeans and two Marys who did not write but loved to read. The seed was growing into a flourishing oak. Sadly in December 2017 Gilbert died. David Bamford suggested an anthology in his memory. Thus our first anthology, and the joint decision to name BRAMPTON POETS, came into being. We now meet in the 'Craft Room' at the Brampton Community Centre on the first Thursday of the month starting at 10am - all are welcome!'.

We have taken poetry into local schools but when Covid came this was paused. However we were not isolated, we wrote three more anthologies, drawing us closer together as a group. Jean Taylor began to write poetry as I did myself. Brampton Poets offers so much to those who join us, bringing their talents and having a platform to create as well as demonstrate their art work in the books.

Ena R. E. Hutchinson

Phil, David and John - three wise Brampton Poets

Promoting Brampton Poets' anthology volume 5

Milton Keynes UK
Ingram Content Group UK Ltd.
UKHW030117061224
452124UK00001B/4